Contents

Alice is starting her game by 'counting out'. It helps to choose who will be 'it'.

She says,
*One potato,
two potato,
three potato,
four
Five potato,
six potato,
seven potato
more.*

Counting out is a very ancient custom.

Ip dip do,
Cat's got the 'flu
Dog's got measles
Out goes you!

In Scotland seventy years ago, children said:

Yan, tan, tethera, methera, pimp,
sethera, lethera, levers, dovers, dick.

Sheep dipping by Margaret Baird

Shepherds used the same words when they counted their sheep.

Playing in the playground, Highway School, Chadwell

We can find out about playground games in the past by asking older people what they used to play when they were at school.

What do you say at your school?

What did your Grandma do when she went to school?

These children are enjoying a game of football.

These boys are playing football, too.

Look at their clothes and shoes.

Do you think this is a modern photograph?

Playing football, August 1954

Robert enjoys throwing and catching against the wall.

He says,

> Are you going to golf, sir?
> No, sir.
> Why, sir?
> Because I've got a cold, sir.
> Where did you get a cold, sir?
> At the North Pole, sir.
> What were you doing there, sir?
> Catching Polar Bears, sir.
> How many did you catch, sir?
> One, two, three, four, five ...

Here are some bouncing and catching rhymes which children said in the past.

> What will my husband be?
> Tinker, tailor, soldier, sailor,
> Rich man, poor man, beggarman, thief.
> What should I be married in?
> Silk, satin, muslin, rags.
> What shall we live in?
> Big house, little house, pig sty, barn.

> PK chewing gum, tuppence a packet,
> First you suck it, then you crack it,
> Then you stick it on your jacket.

A sailor went to sea, sea, sea,
To see what he could see, see, see.
And all that he could see, see, see
Was the bottom of the deep blue sea, sea, sea.

Many modern rhymes are based on
what is seen on television.

Children's jobs

Older rhymes often told of the jobs that children had to do.

My mother says I must go
With my Daddy's dinner-o,
Chopped potatoes, beef and steak,
Two red herrings and an oatmeal cake.

What job did this child have to do?

Iron and Coal by Wiliam Bell Scott

I went to visit friends one day,
They only lived across the way,
They said they couldn't come out to play.
Because it was their washing day.
This is the way we wash all day,
  Wash all day,
      Wash all day.
This is the way we wash all day,
Because it is the washing day.

Many children enjoy collecting and swapping things like stickers or badges.

Fifty years ago children also made collections.
These film star cards cost a penny a packet.

Can you make a cat's cradle?

Marie's granny made them at school fifty years ago using an old boot lace.

Ask your granny if she can make one.

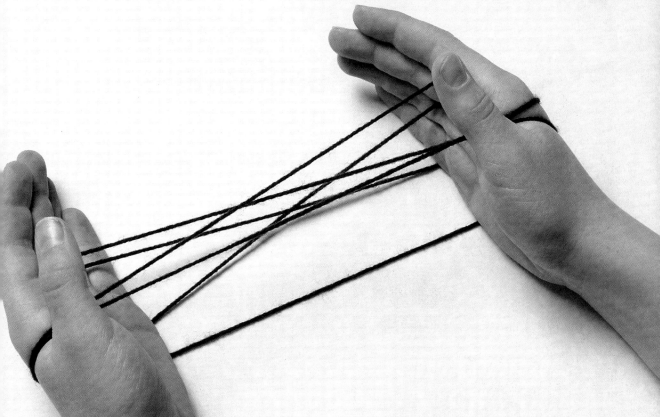

Skipping

Jane's Gran can remember playing skipping games when she was at school.

Her favourite was called "Salt, mustard, vinegar, pepper". The children took it in turns to run in and skip.

Jane enjoys skipping, too.

This skipping rhyme was sung by children thirty years ago in Bedford.

Strawberry, apple,
my jam tart
Tell me the name of
my sweetheart.
A, B, C, D, E...

In Aberdeen they sang:

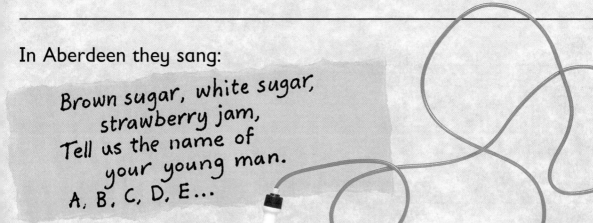

> Brown sugar, white sugar,
>   strawberry jam,
> Tell us the name of
>   your young man.
> A, B, C, D, E...

Which rope do you think is old?
Why?

Here are some older rhymes.

> Mothers in the market,
> Selling penny baskets
> Baby's in the cradle
> Playing with a ladle.
>
> Stockings red, garters blue,
> Trimmed all round with silver,
> A red, red rose upon my head,
> And a gold ring on my finger.
> Tell me, tell me where was I born,
> Over the hills amongst the green corn.

Ryan enjoys playing marbles with his friends.

Each coloured marble has a different value.

Marbles have been played for over four hundred years. The first marbles were made of marble, but now they are made of glass.

These boys played marbles over one hundred and twenty years ago. Their marbles were made of clay.

Some children still like to play jacks. You have to pick up the metal jacks as the ball bounces.

Do you play any of these games?

Children all around the world enjoy playing hopscotch.

Children used to draw the 'bed' with chalk, but this playground has one painted on.

Hopscotch has different names in different parts of Britain: hopscotch, peevers, scotch and ikki dukki.

How can you tell that this is an older photograph of children playing hopscotch?

Playing hopscotch

Children have played chasing games for hundreds of years.
They started when children copied their parents
going out hunting.

'Tig' or 'tag' is one of
Jamie's favourites,
but he also enjoys
'stuck in the mud'.

Which games do you
enjoy?